PROFESSOR FINDS THE PERFECT GIFT

By
Thomas Weatherspoon

Professor Finds The Perfect Gift

iUniverse books may be ordered through booksellers or by contacting:

iUniverse
1663 Liberty Drive
Bloomington, IN 47403
www.iuniverse.com
844-349-9409

ISBN: 978-1-6632-4354-6 (sc)
ISBN: 978-1-6632-4353-9 (e)

Library of Congress Control Number: 2022914205

Also by Thomas Weatherspoon
Professor's Path
Professor Has A Goal
Professor Loses His Joy
Path to Magic~19 Principles of Transformation

Print information available on the last page.

iUniverse rev. date: 08/05/2022

Professor began to think he would never find a gift.
Drudging through each department store as he huffed,
scuffed and sniffed. It was getting close to Mom's
Birthday and he hadn't found a thing. He had a card
but without a gift, what joy would that bring?

Mom always found time to make each birthday special.
Party, clowns and cake were always on the schedule.

He wanted to give her something that would make her feel the

same, and show how much he loved her coming to all his games.
She was always in the stands and he could always hear her voice.

Keeping him motivated and focused, so he could make
the proper choice. He wanted to give her something
that seemed to cheer as loud. A gift that showed

how much he loved her and equally how proud.

His shopping came to an end and he left with empty hands.
Even after spending hours sorting through all the brands.

On the walk home, he decided to ask his Dad. Though he wanted
to do it on his own, he was sure he'd have something to add.
Soon as Professor got home he went straight to his Dad.

He was sure he would get some new ideas better than the
one's he had. "Dad, I m having a hard time finding Mom a gift. I
looked almost everywhere but no matter how hard I persist,

I come up empty handed and left with just a wish." "Don't
worry son," his Dad replied. "It will come to you.

No matter what you get your Mother, she will love it through
and through." But that didn't relieve Professor's mind,

he wanted something grand. With all his Mom had done for
him, something simple was not the plan. He knew his Dad
meant well and he was sure that he was right. But it

didn't make things easier, though he thanked him to be polite.

The next day after school Professor went to
the mall. He was sure he would find the perfect
present. It had been three days, after all.

As he looked around he began to think. Maybe he should try

to make a gift on his own. Something that would
make her smile, laugh and maybe cry.

His Mom was fond of rainbows. She had them

all around her room. There were pictures, puzzles and figurines.

On their bedroom fireplace, a rainbow colored plume.

Now that he had an idea, his energy increased. He promised
himself he would not stop until he found the perfect piece.

In one store and out the next, he searched high and low.

Rushing he heard a crashing sound and a sharp pain

in his elbow. On the ground, a red picture frame he
bumped when he turned around. "Oh no!" he cried
to himself. "How did I knock that down?"

Fortunately the frame was fine. Not a single crack. Just
then an idea came to mind as he went to put it back.

The frame would make a perfect gift
with a rainbow pictured inside.

But he could never draw that picture
no matter how hard he tried.

He placed the frame on the counter top so that the cashier
could ring it up. "My this is a pretty frame," she exclaimed.

To that Professor said, "Yup!" "Oh you don't sound very excited.

Is this for a special day?" she questioned Professor
briefly though he didn't have much to say.

"It's such a lovely surprise. What will you put inside?"

"I haven't worked that out just yet," a sad Professor replied.
"Maybe a picture or a poem but I can't seem to decide."

"I want the picture to be a rainbow high up in the sky. Even
a poem on rainbows, that would make me satisfied."

The cashier was moved by Professor's words and that made
her want to try. To see if she could find a rainbow picture
high up in the sky. She thought about the photographer

who took photos all the time. Usually of parents with their babies.

Just then something else came to mind.

"Come with me young man," the cashier said with a smile.
"I think I have the best thing and it might fit your style."
Professor followed and hoped that she was right.

He thought to himself,

"I want a gift but I don't want to be here all night." When
they found the photographer she whispered in his ear.

He then proceeded to look around but for what just wasn't clear.

Minutes later he returned and was happy
as can be. "I found it!" he shouted.

"I have the rainbow, can you see?"

He rolled out a very large tarp, he was holding in his arms. It was a picture of a rainbow stretched over a small farm. "That's much too big for the picture frame," Professor quietly replied. The photographer and cashier laughed so hard he almost cried.

"Oh no young man," the photographer said. "This will go behind. You will stand right here in front and I'll shoot the rainbow and you combined.

That way you will have a picture under the rainbow, and I can have it placed in your frame before you have to go." This made Professor happy and he couldn't wait to see, what the final product would look like, rainbow, frame and he.

The photographer disappeared and the cashier took him back to pay for the frame that luckily hadn't cracked.

When the photographer returned the frame was polished
he could tell. A huge smiled erupted on his face, the cashier
grinned as well. The picture turned out wonderful.

It was a beautiful rainbow! He knew his Mom would be happy.

The picture seemed to glow.

The cashier wrapped the lovely gift and Professor paid and left.
He was barely out the door when he heard the photographer
out of breath. "Young man hold on a minute!" he heard

the gentleman shout. "I have something else for
you that your picture can't do without."

He passed Professor a scroll on a very old parchment.

It was a gift from his Mom when he was a boy

and it made him feel content. There was a story
and a poem and this is how it went;

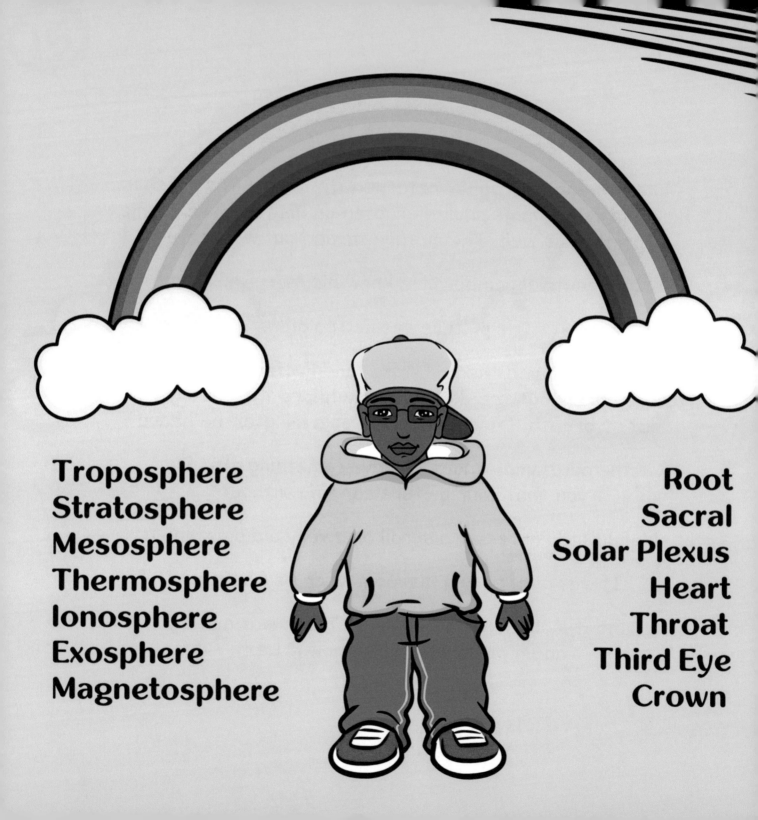

Troposphere
Stratosphere
Mesosphere
Thermosphere
Ionosphere
Exosphere
Magnetosphere

Root
Sacral
Solar Plexus
Heart
Throat
Third Eye
Crown

It took God six days to create the world. On the seventh he took a rest. After each day of creation, he placed a layer of protection, so the design would be blessed.

There are seven layers of protection over all that was made. So that all God's creation would have no reason to be afraid.

Those layers can't be seen but we know they are there. Like the layer that keeps out the harmful rays, or the one

that keeps in the air. From the Troposhpere to the Magnetosphere.

Something powerful placed them there.

We are reminded of the seven layers whenever a rainbow is seen. After the rain when the sun shines again, like a fine oiled machine.

ROY-G-BIV, is how we recall the colors of his gift. God's

way, some would say, of letting us know He exist. Red, Orange, Yellow, Green, Blue, Indigo, and on the seventh day when his head he'd lay, it was Violet that gave him bliss. Seven days, seven layers, seven colors of the rainbow. A colorful blaze, of a silent prayer, so powerfully magical.

But the story is not finished, this final verse is also true. God in his infinite wisdom placed a rainbow inside of you. From the bottom of your spine to the top of your head, are seven layers of energy, the first one is red. These layers are called Chakras

and they allow your energy to flow. God lives inside of us and he wanted us to know. So with the touch of his hand, and with love as the plan, he placed in each of us a rainbow!

Red is your Root Chakra, energy at the base of your spine. Orange, your Sacral Chakra, your emotions and second in line. Yellow is your Solar Plexus where your power comes from. Green is the Heart Chakra, without it nothing gets done.

Blue is your Throat Chakra and gives power to your words. Indigo represents your Third Eye, where all wisdom is transferred. Violet is your Crown and it's at the top of your head.

It is there that God waits for you every night when you go to bed. After the story there was a poem at the end. Professor had to read it a couple of times but he knew his Mom would comprehend.

RAINBOW

Given what I've been told or the folklore that's been written.

I close my eyes as the clouds pass by
and colors start reminiscing.

But because of what's been told I can't be satisfied. Without
its end we can only pretend that the myth is not a lie.

About a colorful path that brings a joyful
laugh as it stretches across the sky.

But at its end is gold my friend that feeds those needs or greed.
And once found there on the ground your happiness can proceed.
But my eyes see it differently as I trace where it all begins.

In the beginning the colors are just as strong,
as there where she finds her end.

The joy released at the start of your path, is a
reward within itself. As it guides your steps with
beautiful rays to guide you to it's wealth.

The next morning he placed his gifts outside his Mother's door. Waiting patiently for her to see the surprise he had in store. The door opened slowly then he heard his Mother shout, "Oh my! someone left me a gift. I wonder what this is about?" "It's for your birthday!" Professor screamed to add to the surprise. When she began to read the story,

he saw tears flow from her eyes. Then
unwrapped the frame with the

rainbow picture and he could feel her joy rise.

"Oh Professor,I love my amazing gifts. The story and poem made me cry. Wherever did you get them from? " she questioned

her little guy. Professor explained, "the
photographer at the store

thought you should have them with your frame. He and the cashier were so very nice and I don't even know their names. I'm still not sure what the poem means though I know it's about the

rainbow. Can you explain it to me? But please go nice and slow."

She hugged Professor tightly as they both began to laugh. "Well it's like your Father taught you about the magic path.

You don't wait to be happy until the job is at it's end.

The magic comes when you're joyful, even before

you begin. That way your happiness is in the effort not only if you win."

Professor whispered, "Happy Birthday Mom." Then kissed her on the cheek and with a joyful chuckle,

he asked "Mom when can we eat."

THE END

Printed in the United States
by Baker & Taylor Publisher Services